Instructions at Sunset

Also by Geraldine Connolly

Aileron
Hand of the Wind
Province of Fire
Food for the Winter
The Red Room (chapbook)

Instructions at Sunset

Geraldine Connolly

Terrapin Books

© 2025 by Geraldine Connolly
Printed in the United States of America.
All rights reserved.
No part of this book may be reproduced in any manner, except for brief quotations embodied in critical articles or reviews.

Terrapin Books
4 Midvale Avenue
West Caldwell, NJ 07006

www.terrapinbooks.com

ISBN: 978-1-947896-85-7
Library of Congress Control Number: 2025939467

First Edition

Cover art: Saguaro National Park
courtesy of Getty Images

for Steve

Contents

I
For Emily	7
Ars Poetica	8
Two Foxes	9
I Want to Bring Back	10
Mayapples	12
Handmaidens	13
Spider	15
Ghost Trees	16
In the Woods as Children	17
My Own Sky	18
Grief's Panther	19
Instructions at Sunset	20

II
Woodpecker	23
The Old Stories	24
Grandmother's Plums	26
We Live Inside the Eyes of Others	28
Dream of the River	29
Tucson Morning, 6 a.m.	30
Summers at the Lake	31
Howard Johnson's, Pennsylvania Turnpike, 1965	32
The Zen of Cooking	34
The Room I Had as a Girl	35

III
From the Far Corner, I Enter the Page	39
Miss York	40
The First Gathering	42
Letter to Joanna	43
Here in My Ruined Garden	44
Cicadas	45
The Great Forest: Max Ernst	46

IV

Faith	49
On Saturday Nights in Greensburg	50
Sawing the Mesquite	51
Spring in the Desert	53
When the Storm Came Up	54
Palo Verde	55
Empathy	57
In Old Sonora	59
All Souls Procession: Tucson	61

V

Her Possessions	65
Gratitude	66
Love Poem after Neruda	67
Ode to Morning	68
Above the Dull and Spiritless World	70
Alma	72
What I Remember About My Wedding	74
Eros	76
In the October Dusk	77
Gazing out the Window in Park City on New Year's Day	78
Returning to Tucson	79
Acknowledgments	83
About the Author	85

I

For Emily

she listened in the hall
seldom crossed thresholds

baked dark cakes
with spirit-soaked raisins

dug with a trowel
at the edge of deep woods

dropped to her knees
to examine a caterpillar

rinsed windows with vinegar

while inside
intrigue twirled and spun

she loved
interruptions

which nothing could silence
or calm or cool

Ars Poetica

>—after Remedios Varo's *Armonia*

Her bed sits empty, the floor unswept
as she works through the blue night.
Trunks remain unlocked and

must be opened, so many ideas,
so many empty myths to transform.
Hurry, she tells herself,
the restless voices are about to fade.

They may escape, like birds,
through the open door
I feel this way about time.
If I don't capture what's
happening in words,

it will disappear. I must see past
the dark in the high windows,
past shadows, into closets

and hurry, for outside, minutes pass,
their wings brush the windows
like muffled screams.

Two Foxes

I watch from my window
as the crystal axe of winter
shatters the yard's blank mask
into luminous frost stars.

Sudden ribbons of muscle and fur,
two red foxes, tails on fire,
erupt from their house of snow.
Across the channel of unknowing,

a restless wish rises, an urge
to escape my body's border.
Across the yard the foxes surge.
The sky lets loose its white shrapnel.

Leaves drown, numbed into tatters.
Wherever I go, I want to leave.

I Want to Bring Back

My organdy Easter dress and straw hat
with a navy ribbon, tight green blossoms
in April, gravestones among apple trees,
the Virgin's long blue robe, the startled ringing
of the altar bell like breaking icicles, that moment
when bread changes into the body of God.

Bring back crocuses and Easter chicks, reborn Jesus,
dogwoods and sycamores, who wore their blazing hats
of ivory. Eggs and lilies, the first moment
the orchard above the farmhouse blossomed
pink above the muddy creek, a ring
near furrowed fields, of apple trees.

Pheasants with wings like helicopter blades, trees
that bloomed, lifting their faces toward God,
the whole of the newly ploughed garden bringing
hints of hope. We tied on our hats
and to the ribbons fastened dry blossoms
with certainty, and that quiet instant

before we prayed became the moment
we wandered, lost among the trees,
muddied our stockings, crushed blossoms
beneath our shoes, cried out to the old God
to save us from falling. I remember that
once we were innocent, once we wore our ring

of belief like a badge, a feeling of being wrung
clean as we prayed, as if we could begin again.
I call to innocence, to girls in Communion hats
about to ascend the steep rows of church steps
to kneel, to bow and greet their God
as dark rows of widows and penitents like blossoms

in the apse lighting candles, their flame blossoms
illuminating the faithful, gathered and singing
songs of praise, hymns to the one God,
our faith restored, all of this in the moment
before mystery approached, belief failed, before trees
of new knowledge grew up into the heat
and fervor of the world. Tight green blossoms,
gravestones in the shade of apple trees, I call and
call to them, although there is no answer.

Mayapples

We children called them
Devil's Apples.

They clustered in woods
we traipsed through

covering mushroom stubs and moss,
spreading their wide cool fans.

In the humid daze of summer
each leaf spread its small umbrella

then divided in half in the woodland drizzle,
dewy and fresh in the loam.

Somehow we never saw the apple,
the poisonous tuber below.

Handmaidens

After we milked the cows, gathered eggs
and hung the wash, we rode bareback
into the meadows of alfalfa
then stormed the woods where the boys
had built a tree fort. We scaled the
rope stairs to the high branches
of a pin oak to challenge them,
grunting, cracking our boards against
their boards, sweating and cursing.

We wanted to prove ourselves in battle,
to slay other brave and beautiful warriors
who belonged to tribes of Nomads,
in the regions of Scythia
where the Chinese built the Great Wall
to hold us back. Great archers,
great riders, beholden to no men,
sisters of the battle, companions,
we would have gladly died together
buried with our weapons.

What is it that compelled us, Carol,
to return home and live in disguise
rising to cook eggs and sausage,
then set the table to serve
our male cousins and uncles.
We worked as handmaidens

but longed for the late afternoon,
when we would set out

again on our journey
pure of heart and purpose
from the Black Sea to Mongolia
with hand-carved bows and
horses we had trained.
I remember you, cousin,
your spear lifted,
hair tangled in the wind.
My fear is that
I have remained a servant.

Now as I watch my granddaughter
reprimanded for interrupting an adult,
for not thinking before she speaks,
I call forth the spirit of those
Amazon girls we once were.
I will her to step forward,
to answer back.

Spider

The one who swings the black star
of its body across the pane,
the one who keeps hanging

a blindfold over the door, spinning
its small hand-lettered invitation.
When I brush it into the grass,

it vanishes. When I threaten it
with the broom's thunder, it
scuttles into shadows.

I check and recheck but somehow
the spider returns, solitary
acrobat of the intricate.

Although I brush it and drench it,
though I pummel the doorframe,
the spider resurrects itself,

eight legs of doom skittering,
a zigzag of yellow
lightning in a sea of charcoal.

Even as I wait for sleep's oblivion,
I watch for it, raising a hand against
the tangled cobweb in my dream.

Ghost Trees

I dreamed we still owned the farm
but the sagging barn had been
covered with corrugated nickel
and the mud and swill with shiny plastic.
The farm was given to me as a gift
and I roamed through the old rooms
filled with discarded sofas,
sagging mattresses, soiled toys.
I'm writing this as I stare
at palm trees almost lost in fog.
I'd trade these ghost trees for the past,
a blurry limb for a clean row of corn.
I'd walk down the road to the creek
and stand under green willows
near fresh creek water
to listen for the rustle of wings,
to watch the small frogs leap.

In the Woods as Children

Remember, how we took off
our clothes among the mayflowers?
How everything was simple, the hours
passed without pausing.

The sun could read our minds
as we ran through the trees
Come back to us, the elms cried out.
As our hands turned to leaves
and our arms became branches
reaching up like arrows into the sky.

My Own Sky

Past the empty vases in the hallway
past the unlit lamp
with its great cabbage roses,
the smell of mothballs and
rusting jars in the dank cellar
past the stacks of yellowed magazines
and old church bulletins, the dried palms
from Palm Sunday hung from the wall clock.

Past the kitchen with mealybugs in the flour
and dead flies stuck on the windowpane,
nothing ever thrown away, nothing
ever sorted, there sat Mother,
after her latest rant, stitching away
on the couch amidst the chaos, her endless
quilt squares scattered on the floor.
Below pink wallpaper at the open window
white curtains floated like untold lies.

Past my room where I had stacked
my books with care on the bookshelf
and lingered on the bed reading,
I remember the tree growing up
across the high window.
Sometimes I reached above
to catch the sky, my own sky,
clear and blameless.

Grief's Panther

Galvanized black, it lay,
blurred, lithe,

then pounced from a boulder
to knock me so flat I could

barely stand.
My father was dead.

If I spoke, it would have
been a moan or a howl.

If I hurried, the panther
would not quit, would run faster.

Go slow, I said to myself.
Go slow and ragged.

Twist with change, breath
that expands and contracts.

Its claws grew longer
against things as they were,

rushed and stumbling,
the fur of the beast matted.

Instructions at Sunset

When the light turns the clouds pink
and shadows appear, when meat
is burning, when a dog licks
his haunches in the dry grass
and a bee climbs into the scented rose,
you may forget your childhood,
forget the grown-ups
gossiping, swigging beer
and lighting cigarettes.

Like someone playing God,
call out to the burning bush
of light. Turn and beckon
the sun toward its final drop
into the charcoal pool of night.
Command the moon to
come forward. Summon
the rest of your life to its feet.

II

Woodpecker

Rising in the half dark
after a night of bad dreams,
I hear the rattle of the fireplace's metal cap,
a windshield at the top of the chimney
where a woodpecker hammers away

broadcasting to the world that
he owns this yard
and is looking for a mate.

Maybe as Slavic folklore goes,
he's also announcing a death.
Infections multiply each day
as I dream of coffins floating
one by one into the sea.

Each soul has left the world,
the woodpecker sounds his drum.
I begin to count the taps
but then fifty, a hundred,
a thousand, and I lose count….

The Old Stories

I'm going back to the past
the way the wren goes back to her tree,
back into the faceless past.
I remember the story of diamonds
sewn into the hem of Grandmother's skirt,
the tale of Uncle hidden among the hay bales,
the story of Stanislaus sent ahead to
find a job in America, then gone back
to bring friends and cousins, to bring
his bride to Pennsylvania.

The old stories, those lost worlds,
those words whispered into the breeze,
twisted like ribbons in the wind.
I never got tired of hearing them,
their danger, their drama.
Back into the faceless past I'd head
like a diver into salty waves,
when one of the aunts would whisper
the Old World names—*Stanislaus, Adela,
Vladja*—they echoed in my ears,
each of the stories always a little changed,
each an ornament
borne by a different character,
so much more colorful than
my dull life in America,

those Old World stories
each told at a different time,
in a hushed voice, changing
in the sleet, in the rain.

Grandmother's Plums

Sitting on the counter
in a big blue bowl
or sliced in half-moons
and spread across a plate,

those purple globes were
worthy of a painting
by Cezanne.

She boiled them down
as in the old country,
into butter, dried them,

chopped them
into hunter's stew
or layered them
through sweet dough.

Their flesh
was tucked inside
a crisp sugar tart
or a baby's pablum,

far away from the past,
from the wars, the flooded
crops, the bombed cities.

Humming at the stove,
she stirred with a large spoon,
forgetting her long journey,

now in America with its
flickering possibilities,
a handful of plums in her pocket.

We Live Inside the Eyes of Others

as we peer into mirrors,
apply eyeliner and blush, change
our socks or hat to make a statement,
consider an effect we want to create.
The mirror acts as the eyes of the other,
what hairstyle, which lipstick?

Even the words we speak, the way
we speak them, they river into melody,
or sink into oblivion.
We live inside the eyes of others.
My vanity is a cardinal not a sparrow,
my vanity is always hungry for more.
How to appear? What effect?
In his eyes, her eyes, my shine.

Dream of the River

I have only a flimsy bicycle, red with tinny wheels. No plastic bag. And the river is rushing past. No money and no telephone. The waters wash through my eyelids and waves howl like sirens. If I were a wheel I would roll down the road to safety. But I am not a wheel. I am only the rusted brake in a sea of water. I cannot steer to the right or to the left, or even straight ahead. The hard seat doesn't fit quite right. The wheels are too large and the river churns on. The dock disappears, the spokes refuse to turn. I notice flotsam and jetsam and sometimes feel a tremor of hope like a ripple above the fast water, useless as butterflies. I regret I never learned to swim. So I cling to a handlebar and say goodbye to mayflowers, dogwood, abandoned barns, to an endless wave of baptisms, weddings and funerals, a blur of cousins, long tables covered with tablecloths and heavy platters, bowls of fruit, steaming roasts, coffee urns and sheet cakes. Soon the bicycle will sink into the water. My brother arrives in a vision to say goodbye. Soon the breeze will lift me so that I can see the small pebble in the bottom of a birch bark canoe painted with the day of my death, moving toward me in the mist.

Tucson Morning, 6 a.m.

I walk through the neighborhood,
past the ends of driveways,
front doors locked tight.

The day opens like a new recipe.
I want to follow its neat
measurements, solve its problems.
Each breeze stirs a blossom.

I smell something sweet, dusty, earthy—
sage and creosote, a whiff of mesquite.
I find a quail's nest, its small eggs close
to my shoe, like bones about to break.

I often walk, away from the thought
of border crossings, away from breaking
news toward the patient saguaros,
as a babble of doves surges up
from the saltbush.

Summers at the Lake

Strawberries and fried perch,
fresh tomatoes and sunsets,
the glow of kerosene lanterns
across pine board walls,
Gin Rummy or War or Parcheesi.
Thunder clouds sometimes appeared.

We smelled the heavy hydrangeas
hanging from thin stems.
When our parents motored off
in their white boat to catch pickerel,
ripe apples fell, minnows shuddered

and we were alone as I am alone now
remembering, the canoe splintered into rot,
the cabin sunk into its bones before it was sold.
Even my memories have shrunk
into tiny flies that buzz and whine before
they land on me, as they did in Shawanaga.

Howard Johnson's, Pennsylvania Turnpike, 1965

I pinned my name tag onto my right breast pocket
and stood at attention as our manager, Mrs. Worr,
facial tics jerking like bullets, inspected us.
She shoved stray hairs back into hairnets,

scrubbed spots of grease from sleeves,
buffed shoes and straightened hairpins until
we passed muster. We paraded past crazy James,
the dishwasher, his hair rising like smoky wisps

into a cloud of steam. Steel counters gleamed.
The starched linen of the cook's uniform
stood firm. Miss Cross, our hostess, presided,
mahogany-haired, histrionic, at her dining room

command. *Right station*, she barked,
back room—party of six, and led us there,
menus tucked under her arm like campaign maps.
The restaurant, *Pleasant Valley*, was oddly named.

As rows of Boy Scouts descended from buses onto
the counter stools, the soda jerk, George, scooped
mounds of vanilla and strawberry ice cream topped
with whipped cream into the mouths of parfait glasses.

Battalions of customers arrived. I took
a green pad and stubby pencil from my pocket
to write down in code the orders: *hjcola,
two fr chick, spagh, hmbg/ no FF.*

Then I raced back to the fat cook, Clara, in her
chef's hat, who'd slip me a sliver of pie, a cookie, or
a french fry when the manager went out for a smoke.
We hoisted the trays of Buffalo China up onto

our thin shoulders and marched out to face a
phalanx of hungry families. Breakfast shift, late shift,
we pushed *Ho Jo colas* and the day's special, pushed
the door open into a dining room of wild-eyed

enemies with hordes of screaming children.
Seventeen. I was already war-torn, battle weary,
among customers who would leave small silver coins
under plates or, just as often, only crumpled napkins

and greasy bacon bits before they surged in legions,
tailpipes smoking, headlights focused
like the eyes of stallions, onto the highway
and I retreated, preparing for the next advance.

The Zen of Cooking

I am fretting about surgery, dreaming of my scars.
Something has to come from this pain inside me —
a dinner, a story, a bowl of soup. Garlic opens
my throat, slices of ginger soothe my stomach.
I pick up a knife to chop onions and mushrooms,
scatter them like calm thoughts across rice.
It is the miracle of the ordinary that soothes,
the wonder of bread and yeast, the marriage
of lamb and garlic, salmon and dill. It is butter
sizzling in the pan, onions turned into caramel crescents,
a ripe mango that offers up its sweet flesh.
I need to cover my needles of anxiety
with the gravy of effort. I need to soothe
my nerves, drizzle them with a sweet glaze.

The Room I Had as a Girl

I treasured that tiny dormer room.
When I opened the window, my hair blew into the night
and across the yard above the howls of beagles

as the moon splintered, the wind creaked.
Insects spoke to me, birds knew my name.
Beneath a wool blanket my flashlight shone,

lantern by which I read through the night, hungry
for stories. There was no broken glass,
no tanks and coffins, no boys going off to war.

I loved being snug in that room, while outside
wild onions grew among prickly fir trees, briar roses.
The rumbling of trucks from the interstate echoed.

Cooing doves, everyday birds made their
daily music on the patio rinsed with rain.
Nothing sparkled yet nothing was dim

there in the tangled paradise, my own.
Not yet a death. Not yet a funeral.
Where daffodils rose up like lions.

III

From the Far Corner, I Enter the Page

with my spear, my terror,
irreverence my talisman,

no vista to contemplate,
no stream to refresh my thirst,

only the dry river of myself,
the river's unfurling,

skirting shallows of inertia,
mudflats of narcissism.

I make my way through spare hamlets,
across treacherous ridges,

enduring switchbacks and ledges
to fight confusion.

The story I tell
shifts and unsettles
as it unspools

until dusk flattens into water
and I can finally see.

Miss York

She's a barfly, a real slut, hissed my mother
noting Miss York's nightly pickups of drunk men
at Jacktown Bar. But all I saw the next morning

was my lovely second grade teacher
with the halo of silver-blonde hair,
wearing a pale mauve sweater made

of some soft yarn, like angora, wishing us
all a good morning and a hand clasp.
We could sit on her lap, she would trail

her fingers softly over the locks
of our hair, tickle us under the arm
until we laughed out loud.

She was our Aphrodite, having risen
from the sea foam to grace
our classroom in a human form.

When I think of her she was dressed,
as if for a party, in a white and gold sheath,
her ears adorned with golden hoops.

She sat atop her desk to face us, dangled
her long slim legs in silk stockings,
her nails enameled with *Paint the Town Pink*.

The scent she carried, of roses
and chalk dust, pleased us.
She pulled out a compact

and powdered her nose, swayed her hips
as she walked us out to the playground.
She called me sweetie.

The First Gathering

We look up from our wineglasses,
notice the shadow of a sharp-shinned hawk

near orange blossoms hung from the swag of leaves,
a table covered in green oilcloth with hibiscus

and the baby on her knees on the deck
pushing a toy and making soft noises, our laughter

above platters of mezze warm in the sun, stripes
of sunlight and then shadow across the table

as we notice the dark mass hung from its claws
the round furred body and the tail swaying

as the hawk drags it above the fence post toward
our party as we all stop chattering and

look up, struggle to make
sense of the sharp thuds, fluttering wings,

the dead kitten hung from the hawk's claw,
that dark mass, impossible as grief

that comes out of nowhere on a sunny afternoon.

Letter to Joanna

I wanted to call and tell you I just heard
that a Baltimore bridge collapsed,
but then I remembered that you are dead.
A river passed your old house
where we had parties. Once I made
a Genoise cake, we read our poetry to each other.

We visited a psychic to access our past lives.
I was the wife of a farmer in Virginia,
standing in a window near a blue vase
waiting for his return from war.
I am still waiting at the window for you
to reappear. I don't think that
there is only this one world.

You were my bridge to other worlds.
I wonder which one you might live in now:
a mountain top, a deep hollow rich with weeds,
a forest with a fox I see that is just now
coming through the light, the one
I whistled up, as if it were you.

Here in My Ruined Garden

All day long
the undergrowth spreads.

Terrible flames
of sunlight have set
the weeds on fire.

If I could only find my macheté,
I could hack my way out.
I could cut down
the screaming thorns.

Here the lizards wear collars
and scurry among rocks
like escaped prisoners.

Leafy spurge, buffelgrass.
Chained wings flutter
from nettles.

Even the gardener wears
a black hood and carries
a long sickle
engraved with my initials.

Cicadas

They leave their wings
in the high branches.

Their husks hang
like torn shirts,

cast-off barques afloat
in weedy grass.

You, they ask,
Have you — ever —

after a long wait —
been ready?

From death ships
their ruby eyes
now stare.

Once their mating calls
jackhammered

and their wing whir
made me hold

my hands
to my ears.

The Great Forest: Max Ernst

Beyond the great forest lies
a sky the color of bruised doves.
Trees like fallen skyscrapers
fill the scarred woods.

Among exploded bark,
lopped trunks twist and
pause like massive legs
of mahogany draft horses.

The tree trunks lean on
each other, tilted, askew.
In one of them a bird
still exists. No leaves or dew.

A circular ring floats
like a mirage, *an eye opening,*
white and eclipsed behind
the forest's gloom.

Now I see it. The bird is lit—
a nightingale imagining
quiet days when
the war is over
and the small animals who hide
beneath the underbrush
are ready to be reborn.

IV

Faith

A great smooth lake
where no birds float or dive,
no boats ruin the waves.

Like a great pothole filled with silver,
it emanates silver. A sky of silk, it is
without tears or bloodstains.

A mirror that's always still and alone,
sitting in its plush box
untouched, waiting for thunder.

On Saturday Nights in Greensburg

We cruised in our mini-skirts, my wing girl
Linda and I, in our cat-eye sunglasses,
puffing on Marlboro Lights,
radio scream above the street noise,

singing till we shrieked. We were
all about cars, nothing floral or dreamy,
just hard edges and Mopar hubcaps,
sharp fins and slant-six motors.
Mine was a gold Plymouth Valiant
with a roll-down top, sleek and crisp.

We danced dirty at the Red Rooster Club
with teased hair and hitched-up hems.
We picked up older guys and let them
take us to the drive-in and order
a thick milkshake and Brawny Lad Steak.
Always driving somewhere, to God knows where.

God knows, said the nuns. *He's always watching.*
We were looking for a chrome burst of
excitement. We loved neon and nighttime,
the day long gone, as we shook loose
onto the highway for rock 'n' roll joints,
racing against that white ball in the sky,
sassy, bad-assed, flooring it,
knowing we'd never die.

Sawing the Mesquite

For months it's been an eyesore,
the giant mesquite,
mistletoe-choked, dying.

When the tree men arrive,
buzzing saws tear into
the blackened branches,

strew blighted leaves
and abandoned nests,
set perching birds to scatter,

I wish I could cut
away my own blights
as easily, my urge

to snap back at my mother's
careless remarks, the day
I slapped her when I was

a teenager, raging
at her question about
where I'd been, with whom.

The blackened tree
leans to the side
as it grows smaller,

its shape distorted
like a tumor shaved
by the surgeon's knife.

The buzzing.
The falling.
The carrying away.

As if the misshapen twigs
and dark wings of yesterday's
mistakes could flutter away,
the spider webs of nightmares
disappear,
my angry strikes at my mother
tossed into a pile
and swept away,
the rinse of fresh green
emerging, forgiveness

even though she's gone now,
a possibility
in the shining air.

Spring in the Desert

More than warm winds and orange flames
flickering from the tips of ocotillo,
more than new rabbits and cactus wrens,
it's the shock of the morning sun
knifing through the clouds that
stuns me. Mesquite and ironwood leaves
erupt, lupines and poppies brandish blossoms.
The desert, once bare and fragile, once brown
with winter's crust, is suddenly all riotous blooms.

Spring arrives like someone's kicked off
a festival. Carpenter bees buzz around palo verde,
newborn lizards scuttle across sandstone.
Mourning doves burble and coo.
I can leave behind the humdrum of winter,
its bruises and disappointments. Our yard
is filled with the hope of littered seeds.
I am ready for the business of beginning
anew. Milkweed open their tiny buds as if
to say, *It's possible, I too can change.*

When the Storm Came Up

When the wind blew fifty miles per hour,
I gathered cushions and small succulents
in tiny pots and brought them inside.

While the branches waved wildly,
our mesquite tree leaned into the eaves
and the wind bore a tablecloth into the sky.

I picked up a small broken sapling.
I had warm shelter. I had soup and milk and eggs.
While the wind raged, carrying tumbleweed and

garbage cans into the street, knocking over ant hills,
while hospitals filled with new patients and
body bags from battle were carried to airplanes,

I saved a small tree. I clipped its torn limbs and took
them to the trash, tied the bare trunk of a sapling
around a piece of wood and made a knot. I watered it.

Palo Verde

I see one blossom at the far tip of high limb—
            a thought of enlightenment.

Each of the five green trunks expands
            like a crooked truth.

Each branch, hard and gnarled,
            erupts from the center.

The cactus wren loves the middle branch.

He is the only tenant and
            perches there, a stiff ornament.

The tree shelters the aloe and the gopher plant,
            the ground filled with brittle leaves.

A wren that had taken the middle way
            explodes in a tumult of feathers.

The branch makes a soft green river—

a tree is nothing next to the mountain,

as the weight of the bird
            is nothing next to the branch.

And the soul, both the tree's and mine,

is even less, almost nothing,
       yet it is everything.

Empathy

begins here in the dark
in the unfamiliar house
with its shrouded chairs
and stacks of unread mail.

You search for chocolates
hidden in high cupboards.
You stumble toward a night table
with its crumpled Kleenex,
smudged water glass, half-read book.

You hesitate then climb into the bed
and dream another's dreams,
the baby abandoned
next to the ocean,
the car that can't be found.

You almost recognize
a pile of date pits
next to the bed,
soiled clothes crumpled
on the floor.

You rise to make coffee
and eggs, read the news.
Someone else's life
bewilders you.

Staring into emptiness
as you leave, your body
barely fits through
the door.

In Old Sonora

There's no O'odham word for wall,
only the tall saguaros
standing like lonely
sentinels with nothing to guard

but jumbles of sage brush,
thorny mesquite,
the tiny burrows of voles.

A cactus wren weeps
among steel posts set in concrete
where ancestors sleep.

The old ones walked
back and forth freely
from their new homes

to visit family in the South.
Today, border guards
stop families and divide them,

take the children to a pen.
As the wind keeps blowing
back and forth, back and forth,

it remembers the way ancestors
walked to their birthplaces
to celebrate, to mourn

and then walked back home
because there was no wall.
There was not even a word for *border*.

All Souls Procession: Tucson

We pass by with cherry baskets
and rifles, with hilarity and solemn purpose.

We pass by in wagons and baby carriages,
walking the street this night, dangling holy cards,

waving ragged banners. The men in long
beards join dancing ballerinas.

Nuns pass by and dictators with giant heads,
and rattling carts filled with bones.

We pass wearing tattoos of our loved ones,
next to the red angel with feathered wings,

the great god Ra, the flaming serpent,
the convicts dragging their chains.

I salute the mute stone lions,
the coffin filled with endless photographs

of foot soldiers, stillborn babies.
We march in the parade as if we could

erase their disappearance with ceremony.
We pass and they pass, the tanks and the soldiers.

The dead have many champions.
Some wear the hats and cufflinks of the departed,

press flowers from the graveyard into
the linings of their robes. The puppets pass.

Prayers scrawled on paper fill the urns.
They burn into bright flares then are gone.

V

Her Possessions

I don't want the pewter or
the carved oak clocks, not the Staffordshire
nor the heavy gold bracelets,
the ruby pin or the turquoise,
not anything she's touched or anything
she hasn't touched, her white hair caught
in the sofa cushions, her rusty promises
clogging the faucets. Everything
in that house was chipped or broken,
surviving beyond its beauty,
and the ditches of the farm road
were covered by weeds while
the apple orchard rotted next to
a crumbling spring house.

Even the quilts pieced by hand,
stitched with repeated motifs,
burn them in a bonfire or place
them in a stranger's hands:
Hour Glass. Hole in the Barn Door.
All Tangled Up. Dogtooth Violet.
Crown of Thorns.

Gratitude

Each evening we watch the sun
preparing to leave the mountain.

Red brushstrokes pass over hard stones
as the wind passes over wild broom

and sweeps seeds into darkness
above the formation called Finger Rock.

A bobcat emerges from the mesquite's shadow.
I am indebted to him and the mourning dove

cooing on the wall, the chattering quail,
her eggs in the clay pot and the white toad listing

along the sandstone. There is no gratitude enough
for the rabbit's leap or the lizard's rush

up the adobe wall. I have only thankfulness
for desert rain, the blooming ironwood

and the sky's pink and black pillars of fire.

Love Poem after Neruda

I don't love you as if you were a rose, a topiary
or a flight of crows who propose war,
I love you as if all certainty has fled
secretly into the shadows of the elms.
I love you like a plant that has no flowers or leaves,
the light of the blue petals glowing and
thankful that love lives obscurely within it.
Because I love the smell of the earth,
I love you with no restraint, no regrets
without knowing there is any other way.
Thanks to you, in secret I am reborn
with only the closeness of knowing how
and when. Your hands search me
and my eyes close as if I've gone blind.

Ode to Morning

Find the red flower
and the hummingbird hovering
Find the sucking bee
inside the tiger-colored blossom

Don't close your eyes
Find the berry below the leaf
Find the forest
and the fox's den hidden beneath
a boulder in the forest

Find the stacked stone wall
and the tremor inside the wall
and all of the tiny insects
that thrive there

Find the stray seed
that turned into a melon
the first shoot of a pepper
pushing up from the mud
a vole burrowed beneath
the mass of sun trumpets

If you find the owl
perched on the branch
listen and wait
And if you hear the frogs
don't move

Soon the coyote
will come howling
down from the mountain
and the flower
will wave
its face on fire
with the morning sun

Above the Dull and Spiritless World

sits a woman who made doors for the squirrels,
the man who fed steak to rattlesnakes,

the hostess who served dessert as a first course
surrounded by statues of beribboned lambs,

the painter who wore a priest's collar and donated
his forgeries to the best art museums.

A Dolly Parton look-alike in a flag t-shirt
and striped leggings wanders the Safeway.

That Harley-Davidson rider places his tiny chihuahua
on the handlebars, in a tiny vest, wearing goggles!

Even if you grow a beard down to your knees
or dress your dogs in tuxedos for dinner,

even if you wear a paper Burger King crown
and proclaim yourself the emperor,

I cherish you, eccentrics of the world.
Nothing dull, drab, or lifeless lives in your domain.

You have taken your difference
and treasured it like a newborn.

You have waved it like a proud banner
above the bored and spiritless of the world.

Alma

Outside, even the sky looks amazed
as the moon goes down, as the stars begin to wake.
Our anniversary dinner. We sit on a leather banquette

holding hands among crystal glasses and candlelit stone,
perfect pieces of monkfish arranged across a bed
of pebbles. I place my napkin across my lap

and lift foie gras with apple to my lips.
I sip wine and admire my husband enjoying
salted cod in coriander broth, seaweed, celeriac,

below the glow of hanging lamps that light up
Portuguese Sole and Alentejo Chorizo. Just yesterday
we were irritable and unkind. The word *alma*

means kind, or nourishing, as in our long years of love,
as in the food that is brought on black lacquer
trays on this perfect evening in Lisbon

after a long walk, candlelight and vinho verde.
He whispers, *I'm tired. I want to get back.*
I want to stay. So we devour dessert and coffee,

raise our glasses in forgiveness, sated,
before we head out into the cobblestone street
with its yellow trams, blue tiles, and a mosaic

inside an alcove, a bird with a berry in its mouth.
The streetlights look like transformed moons.

What I Remember About My Wedding

My mother cried the whole time.
When my father walked me down the aisle,
my lower lip trembled as we passed my sobbing mother.
My bridesmaids each carried one red rose.
Their dresses were purple. No, pink. I can't remember.
My brother-in-law was so hungover he nearly fainted.
Purcell's "Wedding March" blasted from the organ
so loudly I almost stumbled and tore the gown hem.

The kiss of peace was a New Age ritual no one knew.
People fumbled, blew air kisses or pumped each
other's hands, embarrassed. No one wanted to kiss
the stranger sitting next to him.
What was that? they mumbled.

I struck the word *obey* from my vows.
I wanted to choke my best friend Nancy
who forgot her slip and refused to walk down
the aisle, delaying the wedding for thirty minutes.
My husband-to-be, soaked with sweat,
thought I'd left him at the altar.

We had a new priest because the one
we'd arranged for left the priesthood.
My boss and his wife gave us
the ugliest candy dish in the universe,
a blown-glass orange bird, its high tail
reaching up like a bad joke to the ceiling.

We didn't have enough finger sandwiches.
My brother and sister-in-law never showed up.
But none of it mattered, and I packed up
the orange bird in tissue paper,
fondly, before we took off for Canada.

Eros

Perhaps he serves as puppet master,
lifting the arms of the lonely into love,
or he's a laughing trickster who
pretends to be a waiter. I've met him a few times
and always, he is unexpected—the director
of an epic film in which the leading man and I
have the starring roles, bemused grins,
hair wild and tangled. He makes the air around him
blossom into neon and makes us believe that this
fever is one we alone have invented.

In the October Dusk

In the high field
where we once walked
through the apple orchard's
sweet blossoms,
I greet you now.

It's still late afternoon
and a tawny glow like honey
spreads across wheat fields
past the dried cornstalks
and cracked leaves of
the soft beds of deer.

Soon the gate of night
will swing open,
and the chill
of darkness will pierce
the gathering clouds.

Soon oak leaves will
flutter down,
cast their dim glow
across your lambs that are
so silent, so watchful,
so carefully carved
onto the headstones.

Gazing out the Window
in Park City on New Year's Day

To my right
the white birch rises
next to a giant pine.

Beneath the lowest branch
the five eyes of the birch
stare back at me.

A magpie lands on it
like a resolution.
The snow is pocked

with the droppings of animals.
I watch the snowman's
red scarf blow in cold wind

like a whisper of death.
Perhaps death is something
we should not fear

but watch rise
and almost touch
the white birch.

Returning to Tucson

Afternoon. The smell of salvia,
seed pods of Texas ebony scatter.
Saguaros descend the hillside.

We will live here until we die,
but in the meantime, the lizard
will leave his burrow beneath

the large white rock, traverse
a sandstone patio, climb a stucco
wall, and slither, into cool shade.

At night the small white
toad creeps from beneath
a palo verde.

Last night I dreamt of a snake
curled inside a boat's prow,
dim in the distance, moving away.

There's no water here, only sandy soil
and rock-faced mountains. Inside
the dry hillsides are black springs,

the afternoon smell of salvia,
dry seed pods of Texas ebony.
We will live here until we falter,

one spring for each spirit
and when we leave, may it be
as jackrabbits leaping the canyon.

Acknowledgments

Aji Review: "Grandmother's Plums"

Anacapa Review: "First Gathering" (as "First Gathering After the Pandemic")

Anti-Heroin Chic: "The Great Forest: Max Ernst," "Spring in the Sonoran Desert"

Blueline: "Summers at the Lake"

Chautauqua Literary Journal: "Dream of the River," "From the Far Corner I Enter the Page," "Two Foxes"

Innisfree Poetry Review: "Empathy," "Handmaidens"

I-70 Review: "Miss York," "Saturday Nights in Greensburg"

Mezzo Cammin: "I Want to Bring Back"

Mom Egg Review: "Her Possessions"

The Museum of Americana: "All Souls Procession: Tucson"

One Art: "Eros"

Poetry Breakfast: "Tucson, 6 AM"

Presence: "Above the Dull and Spiritless World"

Rise Up Review: "In Old Sonora"

Rock Paper Poem: "Alma"

Rogue Agent: "Here in My Ruined Garden"

San Pedro River Review: "What I Remember About My Wedding"

Schuylkill Valley Journey: "Cicadas"

Summerset Review: "Instructions at Sunset"

SWWIM: "Dear Emily," "The Room I Had as a Girl"

Thimble: "The Old Stories"

Twelve Mile Review: "Sawing the Mesquite"

Westchester Review: "Ghost Trees," "The Zen of Cooking"

West Trestle Review: "Gratitude"

What Rough Beast: "Woodpecker"

Your Impossible Voice: "Spider"

Zocalo: "Grief's Panther"

"Dear Emily" was reprinted in the anthology, *Poets Speaking to Poets*, eds. Robert Hamblin and Nicholas Fargnoli (Ars Omnia Press, 2021).

"I Want to Bring Back" was reprinted in *Autumn Sky Poetry Daily*, March 28, 2021.

"Faith" appeared in *Without a Doubt*, ed. Raymond Hammond (NYQ Books, 2025).

Deepest thanks to Natasha Sajé, Tom Speer, Jackie Newlove, Marilyn Halonen, Sally Brandon, and Connemara Wadsworth.

About the Author

Geraldine Connolly is the author of four earlier poetry books, *Food for the Winter*, *Province of Fire*, *Hand of the Wind,* and *Aileron*. Her work has appeared in a variety of literary journals, including *Poetry, Shenandoah,* the *Georgia Review,* and the *Gettysburg Review*. She is the recipient of two NEA fellowships, a Maryland Arts Council fellowship, and a Cafritz Foundation grant. Her work has been broadcast on WPFW radio and featured on Garrison Keillor's *The Writer's Almanac*. She was executive editor of *Poet Lore* from 1994 to 2000 and has taught workshops for the the Maryland Poetry-in-the-Schools Program and the Graduate Writing Program at Johns Hopkins University in Washington, DC. She now lives in Alameda, California.

www.ingramcontent.com/pod-product-compliance
Lightning Source LLC
Chambersburg PA
CBHW030531080526
44586CB00011B/393